# RAISING REAL FATHERS

## AFFECTION

*Book One of a Five Book Series About Fatherhood*

*BY PRINCE-ALBERT*

Print information available on the last page

Rev. date: 11/03/2015

To order additional copies of this book, contact:
Xlibris
1-888-795-4274
www.Xlibris.com
Orders@Xlibris.com


To order additional copies of this book directly from the author contact:

Prince-Albert W. Hudson III
Email: RaisingRealFathers@gmail.com
Website: RRfathers.com

This book is dedicated to my son.


Prince-Albert William Hudson IV

*Its easier to build strong children than to repair broken men-------F. D.*

*It is a wise father that knows his own child. ------W. S.*

# Forward

## Who Am I?

I was raised by a family of strong black women. Some were lovers, but most were fighters. I started life with a father in the home, but due to his military career and my parents' ever changing relationship status, I spent the majority of my youth without him. During the time my parents were together, we spent a lot of classic father-son moments together, like how to fix a flat, ride a bike, play sports and how to fight. These moments helped make me the man I am today. I can say I had it rough growing up without him, but many of my friends had it worse, not knowing their father at all. My lack of manly knowledge left me figuring out how to be a man the hard way. I can remember him telling me I was a leader and not to be a follower, but as a teen, when I needed those words the most, he wasn't there to remind me. Trying to figure it out on my own had me running the streets and making money in whatever opportunity came up. Legal was never the question as long as it had a decent payout. I soon found myself in the back of police cars and in court fighting for my freedom more than just a few times. Many of my friends who didn't have a dad thought court and jail were just part of life, but I knew different. As I grew older, I realized that my friends who had daily interactions with their dads seemed to have a clearer and smoother path into manhood, while my other friends seemed to just take life as it came. There were times that I knew better, but with no father around I took the advice of the males around me. Most of them were adults, but not men by far. Many of them (who were related to me) were hustlers, pimps, drug addicts, bank/jewelry store robbers, boosters and con-artists. Listening to them and the guys in the street had my idea of normal all messed up. As an adult, I re-established my relationship with my father, which gave me the knowledge and drive to become the man I needed to be in order to raise my son properly.

## What can you expect?

The "Raising Real Fathers" book series is designed to mold our young fathers into men who can properly raise boys into real fathers in today's society.

"Affection," the first book in the series, will show that the love between a father and his son is limitless and has few boundaries (if any), which is contrary to what many men may think. I get so tired of hearing that kissing or hugging your son will make him soft or a punk. With so many homophobic men in the world, there is a belief that cuddling or sleeping with your son will make him gay or like men in an undesired manor. These thoughts are nowhere near the truth. Refusing to nurture a boy will only make him a cold individual that doesn't know how to give and receive love. On the other hand, you can't blame narrow minded men because some have never had a father to nurture them. A child is a child regardless of their gender, and children are to be nurtured. I have owned the responsibility of re-teaching our young fathers about the affection and the connection they should share with their sons in the book you are about to read.

# Raising Real Fathers

# Show Physical Love

Show your baby boy love through hugs and pats on the head and back..... from high fives to head butts, physical touch is the first connection you will share with your son after he is born. Everyday your son will learn more; but in the beginning, the only language he will understand is love. Touch your son often! Pick him up and play with him! If he is very young, make sure your hands are clean! If you are a smoker, make sure you change your shirt and wash your hands before holding your baby boy if he is still an infant. Talk to him often, even if he is at the age where he doesn't fully understand what you are saying. When a baby hears a voice on a regular basis, he can find comfort in it; this is another way to show physical love. When you talk to your son, let him know how proud you are to be his dad, and how you will always protect him. It is okay to just hold him and say nothing at all. Staring into your baby boy's eyes will also help form a deep connection. There is no such thing as showing your baby boy too much love or time. The connection a boy has with his dad starts at the beginning of his life and the more time you spend with him the closer you two will become. Don't wait until he is a young man to find out who he is on the inside.

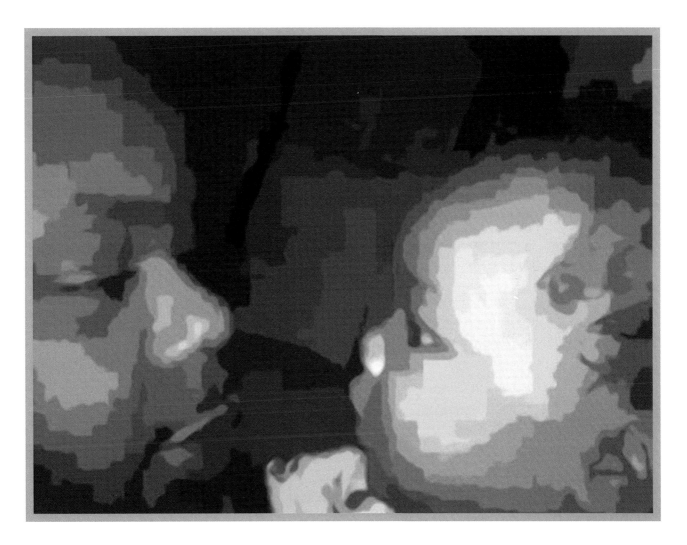

*I still wish I had a dad that was not only around, but involved; Another role model to teach me what my mom did her best to instill- values like hard work and integrity; responsibility and delayed gratification- all the things that give a child the foundation to envision a brighter future for themselves.------B. O .*

# Soft Touch

We all want our little boys to be tough, strong and rugged men one day; but we have to remember that they are still closer to being babies than being men. Our sons will respond better to a softer, gentler touch. Babies and toddlers are to be handled gently. Being rough with a baby or toddler can make them eventually fear you. Babies are very delicate, so take your time when handling them. Their fingers, limbs and joints can be damaged very easily, so make sure you are careful when you are dressing or bathing them. Pay close attention when you are sliding their legs and arms through the sleeves of their clothes; a finger or toe can get hung up in the process, which may lead to serious injury. When you feed him, remember to only give him food that he is ready to digest. Even baby food comes in stages based on their age and what their young stomachs can handle. Feed him in small portions, and keep in mind that they can choke/throw up if they are fed too fast or in large amounts. Surprising a baby can startle him, which can make him uncomfortable. Even though they are young men in training, baby boys need to be cuddled and cared for just as delicately as little girls. You want a soft touch because you don't want to surprise your son too much and make him afraid of you. We often get caught in the thought that boys are tougher and should be treated rougher; but a baby is a baby. Babies need to be held - and nurtured. When a person is rough with a baby boy, it is possible that the child can become scared and shy away from playing rough/boyish physical games as he gets older.

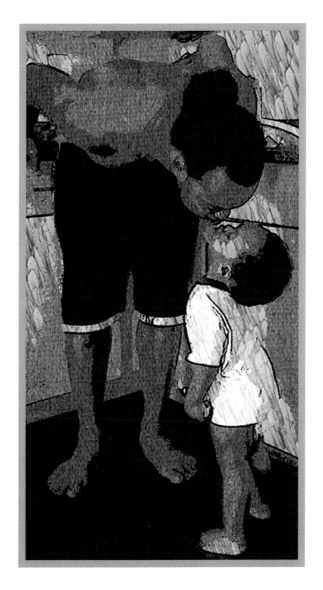

*"Just because you bring a child into the world doesn't mean you're a father,. You have to raise a child, teach him right from wrong, discipline him, put food on the table, put clothes on his back"---- S. O.*

# Sleeping with your Son

Your baby boy's most peaceful times will be when he first wakes and when he is about to go to sleep. Babies are full of energy and might run/crawl all day and night, so the times when they are quiet and sitting still are few and far between. When they are not playing, they are eating. A baby can spend most of its hours breast feeding, so get your time when you can! **A good father should want to be there when he can even if the time is few and short**. These moments often happen when you relax, chill, and sleep with your son**. These are the peaceful times. There is nothing wrong with crashing-out on the couch with your son, even as he gets older and closer to grade school age. Allowing your son to sleep with you creates a deep bond, because you are the face he will see when he goes to sleep and wakes up. If he has a night terror or nightmare (if he is a little older), you will be there to comfort and make him feel better. If you are sleeping overnight, it's a good idea to make sure your son is sleeping higher than you in the bed because "Morning wood" is something that we can't avoid. Making sure your son sleeps up by your chest is a good idea. A dad's chest is a comfortable and convenient resting spot for the baby. Sleeping bare chest to chest with your son can give you two a deeper connection. Resting or sleeping like this, while under a cover, is called Kangaroo/Koala Care because of how physically close you are. BE PREPARED to wake up with a foot in your ear or legs wrapped around your neck. Some babies sleep hard, but it is all worthwhile to be the comforter of your son.

*\*\*Disclaimer (SIDS) or Sudden Infant Death Syndrome is the leading cause of death between infants 1 month to 1 year of age. When your child is within that age range, spend time cuddling/laying with him chest to chest, but if he falls asleep make sure he is moved to a proper laying position inside his crib. In those cases there is nothing wrong with sleeping very close to the crib to maintain that close connection. For more information, research "SIDS" or "Sudden Infant Death Syndrome."*

Like, 'Wow, Dad, you know what, I don't know you, I have no idea who you are, but because of you is part of the reason who I am today.' The fuel that I use—you not being there—it's part of the reason I grew up to become who I am.---- L. J.

# Soft Words

When you speak to your son, remember that he is just a baby. Give him time to learn you and your usual daily routines. People, but more importantly babies, find comfort in consistency. Give your son comfort through consistency. Babies can be easily startled by quick movements and loud sounds. You should try your best not to yell at your baby boy unless he is about to seriously harm himself. The power of a father's voice can stop a child instantly, so use it to your advantage but don't over use it because it can make a child scared of you. You never want to misuse the power you have over your son. **You want your son to feel comfortable with you at all times** - and never scared of you - so speak softly and use soft words, even while they are still babies/toddlers. Babies may not understand all words, but they do feel emotions through the tone of voice we use. I know we want our boys to be tough, but that comes with time! A father's job is to make his child feel secure and protected at all times. This is not possible if your tone scares your boy or if he is scared of your reactions. As your boy begins to talk and understand the world, he will experiment and make mistakes. You want him to feel like he can talk to his dad about anything. If you are quick to yell or get mad, there is a strong chance that your son will not feel this way about you. In fact, he will most likely feel uneasy and nervous when talking with you. A lifetime of father-son talks starts with making your baby boy comfortable through your tone of voice.

*Boys grow to be the father that they never knew------T. C.*

# Patience

We, as fathers, have to take the time to understand our boys. When we do, we allow them to see how they should be patient with others. We have to remember: our boys are still trying to figure out almost everything. (And all Dads are, too) Babies are unsure about lots of things - Everything is new to them! Sometimes boys whine and cry - as much as little girls! Telling a little boy to "stop crying" because "he's a boy, and boys don't cry," makes no sense and it does not make them stronger. We build them up and teach them confidence by being there when they need us. This shows: no matter what happens, Daddy (The strongest man in the world) always has his back; so everything will be okay. We want our baby boys to explore things for themselves, become independent, and to have unrestricted growth. So, we take time and teach them to try/test things out on their own, on their own schedule. While he grows and encounters different situations, we should take time so show him how to approach difficulties with patience. Doing so will teach him that some problems are not easy to solve, and in these cases it takes patience and endurance. Pushing little boys too much can make them, at best, scared and hesitant, even timid; at worst, reckless and self-destructive. Allow your baby boy to move/journey around at his own pace, in his own way. By doing this, you will see the conqueror within and the need to challenge their own limitations will start to come out in a positive way. We want to build boys that know how truly important it is to care about others just as much as they care about themselves.

*Drifting out in space, isolated, far away from the gravitational pull of the earth – just hanging around without direction, nothing to keep me grounded-- no course to run on, no path to follow. That's what it felt like for me growing up fatherless. What I lacked and desperately needed was the strong arm of guidance, that stabilizing, grounding force that only a loving father can give. ---- G. F.*

# Playing Rough!

Ok Dads! You have heard all about love, hugs and all the things you shouldn't do. Now it's time to have fun and teach your son about being tough! **PLAY ROUGH** with your son, but try not to intimidate him. Jump, kick, flip, fall and fall harder. Do whatever you all do to have fun. Make sure you watch for arms, legs and fingers when picking them up really fast. The smaller your son is, the easier it is to accidentally fracture or even break a small bone. I throw my son from one couch to another, sometimes 2-3 feet in distance, but I make sure the couch is clear, even between the cushions. I also make sure I throw him in a way that he won't land awkwardly. Check the furniture for hard spots so he won't land somewhere that can hurt him. If you play rough or wrestle with your baby boy, make sure you watch out for his spine as well. Babies are delicate, but it's our job as men to help them grow into men while keeping them safe. Bear hug your son! Bear hugs are a good way to show him your strength while making your baby boy feel loved and protected. Play indoor soft tackle football using the couch cushions to mark the sidelines. Important! When he falls and cries, it's OK to say "it's OK," and attempt to ease his pain, BUT don't pick him up if it's not major. Let him learn to self-soothe. Let him learn as a little man in training that pain comes and goes. Just get down on one knee so you are close to being eye to eye with him; pat him on the back and rub his head. Try to keep from picking him up in times like these, unless you can see he really needs some love or reassurance that he is protected. As men, we have to allow our boys to experience small pains in a soft way. These are the first steps in building an enduring man.

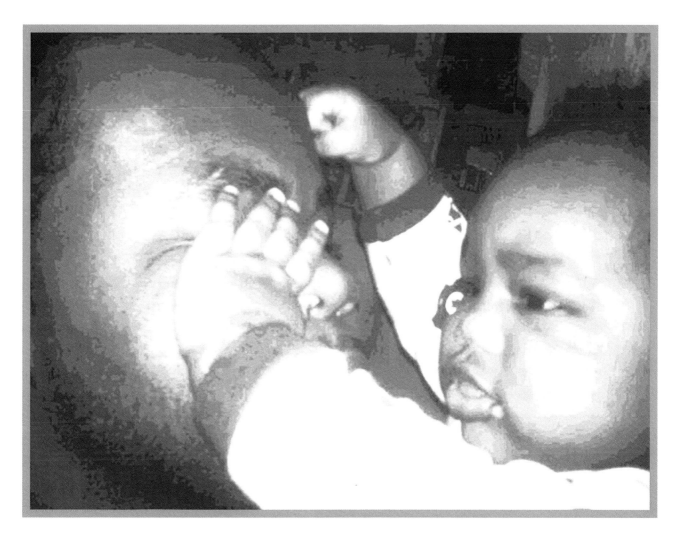

*I ain't come up with no daddy.....If and when I meet him ain't no excuse in the world for why he wasn't there, period! Nothing he can say to that's gonna excuse that. And the way I look at that, my child gon feel the same way no matter what.......me saying i couldn't be there, cause yo momma wouldn't let me, yo mamma had me on a restraining order so I couldn't see you. That don't explain why you didn't call that don't explain why you didn't fight; so no matter what, no matter how many scares you wined up wit when you come up out of this, you gotta keep fighting.. ------------ C. W.*

# Cuddle

Before we can teach little boys to fight, we have to show them how to love - and then what, exactly, is worth fighting for. If we want our boys to be tough and become "Real Men," we have to show them through the way we live. Many men think putting a boy in a fight or flight situation makes them tough, but that is not always the case. We show them tough by being tough, not aggressive. Your son should be able to jump and land in your lap, jump on you, punch you, pull your ears, and know that it is okay. As long as he is playing, he should be able to be tough with you and see that it does not hurt you. "Mind the Jewels!" Rough-housing with your boy, you might find a sudden rush of pain comes in the middle of what is otherwise a great time. We need to show them what a strong man is, not just tell them. Being quick to fight or get loud only makes you seem scary to babies. On the other hand, when your son knows pains that hurt him don't seem to hurt his dad as much, he will strive to be more like that with no pressure. The best way to teach that little boy to be a man is to show him through actions, not demanding what he has to be.

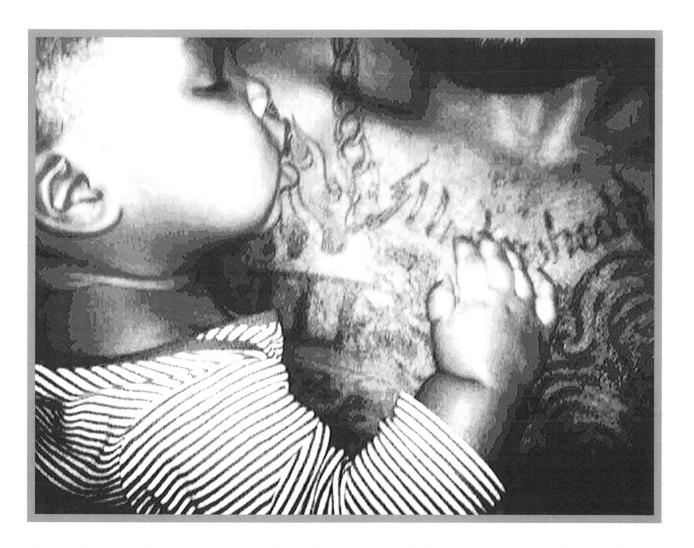

*I never knew my father........I never actually met him.....some people have that thing where they actually want that parent they never had in their life...I have no interest in it. The mistakes I made earlier on, he could have been there to help me not makes those mistakes. ----------C. J.*

# Whining

Babies naturally have soft voices. The obvious reason would be that their voice boxes are smaller; but more importantly, they speak softly sometimes due to uncertainty. Being new to an experience, for example, can make them nervous, which can trigger the soft voice. Being young and uncertain, little boys and girls will whine a lot. Babies should feel unrestricted and free to express themselves in any way they feel comfortable. Self-expression is important. When kids whine, sometimes it's their way of showing they are uncomfortable or in need. It may be as simple as a hug or as major as a sign that they are in pain or getting sick. If a dad is quick to tell his son to "stop whining before I give something to whine about," he might be overlooking an important signal. Take time to listen to them so you can find out what may be wrong. We, as men, often tell little boys to "stop whining and crying and be tough." When we do this, we actually discourage them from expressing their difficulties, driving their frustration inward. Dads teach sons how to deal. We want our little men to feel like they can come to us if they're hurting, comfortable telling us anything. If we over react when they are emotional, they won't feel comfortable expressing their emotions. We only make them feel uncomfortable and more reserved when it comes to resolving the frustration that life brings. Dads teach sons.

*My dad was around for a minute and he bowed out......at one point in my life I had a lot of just honest to goodness hatred in my heart because I felt like he abandoned us, I felt like we wasn't good enough. He went off, got remarried had some more kids, and what about us? That's what I felt like but I don't hold that grudge anymore I think that holding a grudge stifles your blessings. ----------S. S.*

# Take Pride in What's Important

# Part I

There's nothing wrong with wanting a cool son. There's something cute about a little boy who has a big vocabulary. Teaching your baby the latest dance or slang is great but we have to ask ourselves: **"What am I teaching my son? Will this turn him into the man he will need to be in the future?"** We have to promote his native intelligence and curiosities about the world (even if we don't understand them ourselves! - don't be intimidated if your son wants a chemistry set or if your child is strong in a subject area that you know nothing about). **Reward babies for learning and overcoming obstacles, MORE than you reward them for being cool.** A smart boy will grow into an intelligent man. A smart-mouthed boy will grow into a smart-mouthed adult. This is important because we all know some men who talk an excellent game, but have nothing to put behind their words. We have to promote education while they are still infants. Teach them some cool sayings, and some slang, but the key to raising a smart man is getting him used to being educated and educating himself while he is still young. When he is taught to be open to education, he will always be open to making the adjustments that life requires. Little boys need validation in the form of others thinking what they are doing is cool. Whether it is a trophy for education, karate, or basketball, we as fathers have to celebrate their victories and all the positive things that they do.

*My dad was such a good dad that when he left, he left a huge scar. He was my superhero. [I finally talked to him about] what it did to me and asked him why. There was no real answer. There was nothing he could say, because there was no excuse for that. There really isn't. So there was nothing he could say to satisfy me, except to hear me out. And it was up to me to forgive and let go."----S. C. C.*

# *Take Pride in What's Important*
# Part II

We all like to see our boys dressed like little men. I don't know what it is about a well-dressed little boy that can turn even a grown man into a big softy. Whether it is a white tee, Levis and Jordan's, a winter outfit with hat and scarf or a 3 piece suit, the minor details are most important when dressing your son!!! Is your child comfortable wearing what he has on? It's okay to dress your son like a business man in a suit and tie with hard bottoms, but are the shoes good for his feet? If a child is not comfortable, it will show in the way they act. An uncomfortable/unhappy child can change your entire day for the worst. A child's first few pair of shoes should be designed to promote strong legs and posture, not just look good. Sore feet can also make a child unruly. We might prefer ankle socks because they look good but kids need proper socks for support, and when it's cold they need them for warmth. Do his pants fit and are they designed to adjust to his waist? Kids grow in spurts and jeans don't last long. Pants that fit last week could be uncomfortable today. Does his shirt fit well or does it just match well? Never sacrifice what looks good for what fits comfortably. Is his coat too bulky or too thin/thick for the weather? Imagine for a second how it would feel to walk around in something causing you pain, itching or just plain old bothering you, but you don't know how to tell anyone to help you. Then, when a child is whiny or aggravated and crying, some fathers want to get mad and punish the child for "acting up." We should always take time to make sure the materials of the clothes are comfortable. You can watch the way they walk to make sure their shoes fit properly and are not too small/narrow. The younger they are, the more time you will have to take, in order to see what types of clothes are most comfortable and appropriate.

*Being that my father was killed when I was three years old. I don't have a lot of memories of my father. They say you can't miss something you never had.....that's only a little ways right. There have definitely been times as I've gotten older that I've missed my father and, you know his presence not being there. Having someone to ask manly advice, and just things you would ask your father. Also things you would celebrate with him,........that would make him proud.-----S.C.*

# Be Available/Be Consistent

As a father, you should be your sons 911. Imagine for a second that you called 911, and no one came to help... whether your son lives with you or not, it should be easy for him to reach you at any time of the day. If you can't be there in person every time, make sure you are no more than a phone call away. If the relationship with his mother isn't the best, you have to do whatever it takes to keep the peace and keep the lines of communication open. **Any sacrifice is worth being there for your baby boy.** Your son should feel like his dad will always be there and will protect him from anything. This shows him what type of man he should become, and what role he should play when he becomes that man one day. This also gives him a good sense of security. If your son knows that you are there to protect him, he will feel secure. As a man, you know that one day the world will expect him to act as a man would. It is our job as fathers to help them see what they are supposed to be one day at a time. You have to constantly put good information and values in your sons head to make sure he steers clear of attractive distractions that mean him no good. **One of the best things you can show your son is consistency and the best way to show him that is being consistent.** You have to be around in order for your son to see you. Making time for your son will let him know that he is important to you, which is also building good morals by allowing him to see you putting family first. More than anything, you want your son to be very comfortable with you, your voice, smell, sound, and all the things that make you, you. Comfort comes with time. As long as we are breathing, we have time, and time is something all dads can afford to give.

*You tried to make it up, but shit, you couldn't pay enough. You sent me tons of toys and clothes thinkin' you gave enough: But it wasn't though, and you wasn't there. That's all I knew, so I grew up thinkin' you ain't care I know it wasn't fair, but ay, it wasn't fun; But now what's done is done, no matter wha, I'm still yo son-------C. H.*

# Quotes Index

# SOCIAL MEDIA INFORMATION

Twitter
Raising Real Fathers
@RRFathers

Facebook
RRFathers

Tumblr
RRFathers

Instagram
@rrfathers

Personalized and/or Autographed copies are available from the author as well.

Edwards Brothers Malloy
Thorofare, NJ  USA
November 20, 2015